First World War
and Army of Occupation
War Diary
France, Belgium and Germany

28 DIVISION
Divisional Troops
B Squadron Surrey Yeomanry
1 February 1915 - 31 October 1915

WO95/2271/1

Published by

The Naval & Military Press Ltd

Unit 10 Ridgewood Industrial Park,

Uckfield, East Sussex,

TN22 5QE England

Tel: +44 (0) 1825 749494

www.naval-military-press.com

www.nmarchive.com

This diary has been reprinted in facsimile from the original. Any imperfections are inevitably reproduced and the quality may fall short of modern type and cartographic standards.

© **Crown Copyright**
Images reproduced by permission of The National Archives, London, England, 2015.

Contents

Document type	Place/Title	Date From	Date To
Heading	WO95/2271-1		
Heading	'B' Sqn. Surrey Yeomanry Feb-Oct 1915		
Heading	B Squad Surrey Yeo. (Divl. Cav 28th Division) Vol 1-28.2.15		
War Diary	Pradelles	01/02/1915	01/02/1915
War Diary	On the Rome	02/02/1915	02/02/1915
War Diary	Poperinghe (1 mile)	03/02/1915	28/02/1915
Heading	B Squad Surrey Yeo. (28th Divl. Cavy.) Vol II 1-31.3.15		
War Diary	Poperinghe	01/03/1915	28/03/1915
War Diary	Vlamertinge	28/03/1915	31/03/1915
Heading	B. Squad Surrey Yeo. (28th Divl Cav.) Vol III 1-30.4.15		
War Diary	Camp C. Vlamertinge	01/04/1915	10/04/1915
War Diary	Poperinghe	10/04/1915	27/04/1915
War Diary	Vlamertinghe	27/04/1915	30/04/1915
Heading	B. Squadron Surrey Yeo. (28th Divl. Cavalry) Vol IV 1-31.5.15		
War Diary	Farm 1 Mile N W of Vlamertinge	01/05/1915	13/05/1915
War Diary	Hoende Brugge	14/05/1915	17/05/1915
War Diary	Farm 1 Mile N.W. Of Vlamertinghe	21/05/1915	30/05/1915
War Diary	Watou	31/05/1915	31/05/1915
Heading	B Squadn Surrey Yeomanry (28th Divl. Cavalry) Vol V 1-30.6.15.		
War Diary	Watou	01/06/1915	14/06/1915
War Diary	Reninghelst	14/06/1915	20/06/1915
War Diary	Westoutre	20/06/1915	30/06/1915
Heading	B Squadn Surrey Yeo. (28 Divl Cav.) Vol VI 1-31.7.15.		
War Diary	Westoutre	01/07/1915	20/07/1915
War Diary		21/07/1915	28/07/1915
War Diary	Westoutre	28/07/1915	31/07/1915
Heading	B Squadn Surrey Yeo. (28th Divl Cav) Vol VII From 1st to 31st Aug 1915		
War Diary	Westoutre	01/08/1915	08/08/1915
War Diary		09/08/1915	13/08/1915
War Diary		13/08/1915	31/08/1915
Heading	B. Squadron Surrey Yeo. (28th Divl. Cav) Vol VIII Sept. 15		
War Diary	Westoutre Farm M 16c 2.8	01/09/1915	19/09/1915
War Diary		22/09/1915	22/09/1915
War Diary	Merris	23/09/1915	26/09/1915
War Diary	Bethune	27/09/1915	30/09/1915
Heading	B Squadn Surrey Yeo. (28th Divl. Cavy) Vol IX Oct 15		
War Diary	Bethune	01/10/1915	02/10/1915
War Diary		03/10/1915	03/10/1915
War Diary	Beuvry	03/10/1915	05/10/1915
War Diary		05/10/1915	05/10/1915
War Diary	Busnes	06/10/1915	18/10/1915
War Diary	Long Carnot	18/10/1915	18/10/1915

War Diary		18/10/1915	21/10/1915
War Diary		21/10/1915	22/10/1915
War Diary	Marseilles	24/10/1915	24/10/1915
War Diary		24/10/1915	31/10/1915

M0952271/1

28TH DIVISION
DIVL TROOPS

'B' SQN. SURREY YEOMANRY
FEB - OCT 1915

TO SALONIKA

12/4538

R Signal Service Co. (Mot: Cor. 28th Division)

1 – 28.2.15

Army Form C. 2118.

WAR DIARY
or
INTELLIGENCE SUMMARY.
(Erase heading not required.)

Instructions regarding War Diaries and Intelligence Summaries are contained in F.S. Regs., Part II and the Staff Manual respectively. Title pages will be prepared in manuscript.

Hour, Date, Place	Summary of Events and Information	Remarks and references to Appendices
1/2/15 PRADELLES	The last day in these billets. The farms lay very low and there was a big manure heap in the middle of it. The squadron suffered considerably from colds and sore throats. Horses were in the open and the horse lines were very wet. It was very interesting that the townspeople who had been clipped had very much worse throats than horses with their coats all on.	
2/2/15 On the Road	Transport loaded at 6.45 AM Squadron at 7 OAM starting point T roads 300 yds E of FLETRE. March to billets front much impeded by Fr. Tr. especially in STRAZEELE. Days route FLETRE, METEREN, BAILLEUL, LOCRE, ZEVECOTEN OUDERDOM BRANDHOEK to POPERINGHE – RENINGHELST Road. Found the billets a LOFFU Farm was occupied by Middlesex Regt. Had to find new ones.	
3/2/15 POPERINGHE	Excellent barns to billet, cooking facilities good. Water pump (manually pro rest) and from a muddy pond (watering for 6 horses only) the rest in the open. Stables very bad. Approach to Farm (300 yards) where my had from track	

Army Form C. 2118.

WAR DIARY
or
INTELLIGENCE SUMMARY.
(Erase heading not required.)

Instructions regarding War Diaries and Intelligence Summaries are contained in F.S. Regs., Part II. and the Staff Manual respectively. Title pages will be prepared in manuscript.

Hour, Date, Place	Summary of Events and Information	Remarks and references to Appendices
2/2/15 to 1/2/15	Squadron was not employed, except on squadron routine	
8/2/15	Received orders to find No 16 Divisional Mounted Police from the Squadron.	
10/2/15	Instructions received from A.O.C. 28th Division to find one troop per night to march round rear of trenches to discourage snipers. This duty continued till the 19.2.15. Each troop going on duty in the evening and being relieved after 24 hours. No snipers or any evidence of them were found.	
19/2/15 to 28/2/15	Squadron was not employed, except on squadron routine	

121/4808.

"B" Squad Surrey Yeo: (28th Div:l Cav:y)

Vol II 1 – 31. 3. 15

WAR DIARY
or
INTELLIGENCE SUMMARY.
(Erase heading not required.)

Army Form C. 2118.

Instructions regarding War Diaries and Intelligence Summaries are contained in F.S. Regs., Part II. and the Staff Manual respectively. Title pages will be prepared in manuscript.

Hour, Date, Place	Summary of Events and Information	Remarks and references to Appendices
March 1–28 POPERINGHE	The Squadron was not actively employed. Squadron routine, and training hacks (15 men each day) employed the time. Hop poles were found to make very good standings for the horse lines and kept the horses out of the mud. When the hop vines were put out, the horses ate them a little, but no ill effects were noticed.	
March 28 Mar 28–31 VLAMERTINGHE	Harness into Camp VLAMERTINGHE. The Squadron occupied canvas huts, with wooden floors. The horse lines were put down on a clay surface, without a particle of grass. The Squadron continued squadron routine.	

O. Borwick
Major
re. B Squadron Divl. Cavalry
28th Division

12/5140

B. Syrad. levreg fis. (28th Vis lev.)

Vol III. 1 — 30. 4. 15

Army Form C. 2118.

WAR DIARY
or
INTELLIGENCE SUMMARY.
(Erase heading not required.)

Instructions regarding War Diaries and Intelligence Summaries are contained in F.S. Regs., Part II. and the Staff Manual respectively. Title pages will be prepared in manuscript.

Hour, Date, Place	Summary of Events and Information	Remarks and references to Appendices
CAMP C. VLAMERTINGE April 1–10	Squadron routine	
April 10	Went into billets near aerodrome POPERINGHE. The billets were in extremely filthy + 2 whole days were taken in cleaning up.	
POPERINGHE April 10–26	Squadron routine.	
April 23	One officer and 30 men horses were detached for duty with H.Q. 5th Corps. Orders to stand by	
April 27	Moved into billets at farm N.E. of VLAMERTINGHE and about 1 mile from front fence.	
VLAMERTINGHE April 27–30	Squadron routine. Subject still to be stand by orders.	

J. Bonnet
Major
O.C. B Squadron
Surrey Yeomanry
28th Division

121/5481

Reports from units
(28th Divl: Cavalry)

Vol IV   1 - 31.5.15

Army Form C. 2118.

WAR DIARY
or
INTELLIGENCE SUMMARY.
(Erase heading not required.)

Instructions regarding War Diaries and Intelligence Summaries are contained in F.S. Regs., Part II. and the Staff Manual respectively. Title pages will be prepared in manuscript.

Hour, Date, Place	Summary of Events and Information	Remarks and references to Appendices
FARM 1 MILE NW of VLAMERTINGE MAY 1–13	Squadron Routine.	
MAY 14	Marched to HOENDEBRUGGE	
HOENDEBRUGGE MAY 14–17	Squadron Routine	
MAY 17	Marched back to VLAMERTINGE. The Squadron was attached to 3rd Cavalry Brigade for fatigue duties, but was only used once for filling sand bags. Came under the orders of 28th Division again, and returned to the billets NW of VLAMERTINGE.	
FARM 1 MILE N.W. of VLAMERTINGHE MAY 21–30	Squadron Routine. For 36 hours (May 25–26) the squadron provided standing patrols on roads on N.W. of YPRES	
MAY 30	Marched to WATOU.	
WATOU MAY 31	Squadron Routine.	

G. O. Bosweh Major
oc. B Squadron Surrey Yeomanry
28th Division

121/5871

28th Division

"B" Squad'n Surrey Yeomanry.
(28th Divl. Cavalry)

Vol V 1 — 30.6.15.

Army Form C. 2118.

WAR DIARY
or
INTELLIGENCE SUMMARY.
(Erase heading not required.)

Instructions regarding War Diaries and Intelligence Summaries are contained in F. S. Regs., Part II. and the Staff Manual respectively. Title pages will be prepared in manuscript.

Hour, Date, Place	Summary of Events and Information	Remarks and references to Appendices
WATOU Jun 1-14	Division was resting. Squadron Routine	
Jun 14	Moved to new billets 1 mile S.W. of RENINGHELST	
RENINGHELST Jun 14-20	Squadron Routine. Provided 10 men for police. Lieut F G Colman was taken to be camp commandant at DICKEBUSCH	
Jun 20	Marched to new billets 1 mile E. of WESTOUTRE	
WESTOUTRE Jun 20-30	Provided a guard at N.C.O. and 10 men for his cooler supply at DICKEBUSCH. Squadron Routine	for Barnett Major O.C. B Squadron Surrey Yeomanry 28th Divisional Cavalry

181/6214

28th Division

"B" Squad Survey Geo: (SP Dist Coo:)

Vol VII 1 — 31.7.15.

WAR DIARY
or
INTELLIGENCE SUMMARY.
(Erase heading not required.)

Army Form C. 2118.

Hour, Date, Place	Summary of Events and Information	Remarks and references to Appendices
WESTOUTRE July 1 – 20	Squadron in line, had trench digging at night	
July 26 July 27 – 28	Marched to STRAZEELE Squadron engaged in destroying landings which had been rendered unserviceable for use.	
July 28	Marched back to LE STOUTRE	
July 28 – 31 [LESTOUTRE]	Squadron resting and trench digging at night. It was found impossible to continue standing up parties of 30 men nightly to do work in trenches.	

p.o Borwick
Major
O.C. B Squadron Surrey Yeomanry
28th Division

28th Division

/2/
6550

B Squad. Surrey Yeo. (28th Div Cav)

Int VII

from 1st to 31st Aug 1915

WAR DIARY
or
INTELLIGENCE SUMMARY.
(*Erase heading not required.*)

Army Form C. 2118.

Instructions regarding War Diaries and Intelligence Summaries are contained in F.S. Regs., Part II. and the Staff Manual respectively. Title pages will be prepared in manuscript.

Hour, Date, Place	Summary of Events and Information	Remarks and references to Appendices
August 1915. WESTOUTRE		
1st – 8th	30 men working in trenches of subsidiary line every night, and squadron routine.	
9th – 13th	25 men working in trenches of subsidiary line near Dismal Villa every day. And Squadron Routine. No digging. Squadron Drill.	
13th		
13th – 31st	20 men digging daily on SCHERPENBERG, and Squadron routine. During the month great difficulty was experienced with the horses, on account of shortage of men. Horses got fatter, but rapidly lost working condition.	

J.O. Borwick
Major
B Squadron
Surrey Yeomanry
28th Division

12/7016

38th Division

B. Squadron survey pro. (5th Div. Cav)

Vol VIII
Sept 15.

Army Form C. 2118.

WAR DIARY
or
INTELLIGENCE SUMMARY.
(Erase heading not required.)

Instructions regarding War Diaries and Intelligence Summaries are contained in F.S. Regs., Part II. and the Staff Manual respectively. Title pages will be prepared in manuscript.

Hour, Date, Place	Summary of Events and Information	Remarks and references to Appendices
WESTOUTRE FARM M16c 2.8 Sept 1-19	20 men digging daily on SCHERPENBURG and squadron routine	
Sept 22nd	Squadron marched to MERRIS Route St JEAN CAPELLE and METEREN. This route march was independent of the infantry of Division and so merely and completely done	
MERRIS Sept 23	3 subalterns made reconnaissance of roads leading south as far as LA LYS Canal between ST VENANT and ESTAIRES	
Sept 24	2 subalterns made road reconnaissance of roads between ESTAIRES and ARMENTIERES	
Sept 26	Squadron left MERRIS and marched with Div HQ via VIEUX BERQUIN and NEUF BERQUIN to MERVEILLE arrival 12.45 PM and went into billets at REGNIER. 2.10 PM orders received to proceed via PARADIS and LOCON to BETHUNE. Arrived 7.45 PM went into billets	
BETHUNE Sept 27-28-29	at SKATING RINK RUE GENDARMERIE. Standing to, squadron routine	

WAR DIARY
or
INTELLIGENCE SUMMARY.

Army Form C. 2118.

2

Hour, Date, Place	Summary of Events and Information	Remarks and references to Appendices
BETHUNE SEPT 30.	1 officer and 35 men were ordered up to the captured trenches to bury the dead.	G. O. Barnett Major O.C. T.B. attached Army Group any 28th Div. B.E.F.

28th Hussars

D/74/19

"B" Squad: Survey Sec.
(28th Dist: Cav:)
Vol IX
Oct/15

Army Form C. 2118.

WAR DIARY
or
INTELLIGENCE SUMMARY.
(Erase heading not required.)

Instructions regarding War Diaries and Intelligence Summaries are contained in F.S. Regs., Part II. and the Staff Manual respectively. Title pages will be prepared in manuscript.

Hour, Date, Place		Summary of Events and Information	Remarks and references to Appendices
Oct 1-2	BETHUNE	Squadron routine	
Oct 3		marched to BEUVRY.	
Oct 3-5	BEUVRY	Party carrying bombs up to Trenches, day & night	
Oct 5		One party detailed for burying dead at LE CORNET BRASSARD — always 2 a night	
		marched to BUSNES and on to hutts at	
Oct 6-18	BUSNES	March of about 15 miles.	
		Troop Squadron training, including patrols across	
		country. Horses soon learned to clear blind ditches	
Oct 8		Squadron inspected by G.O.C. 1st Corps	
Oct 16		Squadron inspected by G.O.C. 28th Div	
Oct 17		Began information patrols under direct orders	
		of G.O.C. Division	
Oct 18	LONG CARNOY	Marched to LONG CARNOY.	
Oct 18-21		Patrols to Trenches and Squadron routine	
Oct 21/22		Entrained at FOUQUERIE station.	
		Only one ramp for whole Squadron	
		The men very keen and lifted the horses in the	
Oct 24	MARSEILLES	Trucks & proper to lie on the floor.	
		Arrived PRADO station 9 A.M.	
		Unloaded & marched to BARELY PARK. Tents for all ranks	
Oct 24-31		Squadron Routine	

B Squadron, Jersey Yeomanry
Jo Bennett
Major 28th Division

Forms/C. 2118/10.

www.ingramcontent.com/pod-product-compliance
Lightning Source LLC
Chambersburg PA
CBHW081506160426
43193CB00014B/2606